Conten

CW00550901

Contact; mrgerardstrong@gmail.com

Chapter 1

INTRODUCTION TO DATABASES

This chapter is important to read, so that you understand how to plan the structure of a database. However, you may wish to skip this Chapter if you just want to get on with using Microsoft Access 2007

WHAT IS MICROSOFT ACCESS?

Microsoft Access is a data managements system. Databases are used to store large amounts of information, and allow you to store large amounts of data. One benefit of Microsoft Access is that it allows you to find data to provide more useful information.

A database is based on tables of data, and each table contains any number of records (rows).

A recorded has many fields.

See table below for a typical layout for a table of data;

Question 1 How many rows are there in the table?

Question 2 How many fields are there in the table?

Question 3 How many columns are there in the table?

Question 4 How many fields are there in each record?

Customer Name	Date of birth	Location
Bob Harris	01/03/2001	London
Mary Reynolds	17/01/2002	London
Mark Smith	28/09/2000	New York
Lily Grant	21/06/2000	Madrid

Answer 1 There are 4 rows on the table.

Answer 2 Each row holds one record, so there are 4 records in this table.

Answer 3 There are 3 columns. The column headings are the field names.

Answer 4 There are 3 fields in each record – the same as the number of columns

The business owner can use the database to find out information such as;

- **Whether or not he has a customer with a particular name?**
- **Which Customers are from London?**
- **Which location he has most customers?**
- **What customers have the earliest date of birth?**
- **How many customers were born in 2000?**

Databases are not really used for small amounts of data, because the answers to the above questions can be answered easily just by looking at the table. However, if you had hundreds of customers, there would be hundreds of rows, and the table would be so big it would take a long time to answer the questions. This is where a database becomes helpful.

Before creating a database on the computer it is important to plan your database.

PLANNING A DATABASE

When planning a database you need to think about:

What is the purpose of the database?

What information will you want to look up in the database?

What data will you store in the database?

THE SCHOOL TRIP DATABASE

You are going to design a database for a school that is planning various activity weekends for its pupils.

Purpose of the database:

The school trip organiser needs to be able to find out quickly and easily;

> Who is going on a particular activity (for a register)

> How many of the people signed up for a particular activity want transport (so transport can be arranged);

> Contact name and number of a particular member.

After talking to the school trip organiser, you have found out:

> The school is planning 4 activity weekends.

> Each weekend will involve a different activity, pupils can pick from:

- o **Cowboy Adventure**
- o **Cook & Create or**
- o **Mountain Biking**

> The weekend each cost £50 in total.

> The school will provide optional transport from the school to wherever the activity is taking place.

The school needs to have a contact name (e.g. parent's name) telephone number for each member.

Your database should contain details about each pupil and their chosen activity. The next step is to decide which fields to have in your table. Based on the information given above, the table must contain the following information about each member:

- Name
- Date of birth
- Contact Name
- Contact Number
- Chosen activity
- Amount Paid
- Transport required?

This list will be used to decide what fields are needed in your table.

DATA TYPES

Before you can enter the fields into your database, you need to think about what format the data will be in. Access has different data types to pick, which you can see in the table below;

Text	Letters, symbols and numbers, i.e. Alphanumeric data.
Number	Numbers only (no letter at all). Included numbers with decimal points.
Date/Time	Dates and Times
Currency	For all monetary data. Access will insert a currency symbol before the amount (such as £, $ or € etc)
Yes/No	Used wherever the fields can only take 2 values, Y/N, True/False etc.
AutoNumber	This is a unique value generated by Access for each record

DECIDING ON DATA TYPES

You will need to pick a data type for each field from the table 1.2. You must be careful when you plan to pick the correct data type for the field as you will not be easy to change it once you start to enter data into the table.

For example, should you pick a telephone number as a text field or a Number field?

At first you may think that a Number field would be best but in practice this is a bad idea for two reasons;

Access will not record the first zero in a number field. So if the number is 035545300 it will be recorded as 35545300.

Access will not allow you to have a space or bracket in a number field. So you will not able to record a number like this, 01355 599600.

SELECTING FIELDS

We already have a list that will form the basis of the fields in the database (Name, Date of Birth). You may now which to split some of the pieces of information, for example, Name will include a first name and a surname. Should you split this into two fields? There are two main reasons why you may wish to do this;

If you want to sort the members alphabetically by surname, this is much easier to do of surname is a separate field.

You may want to search for a pupil's record. It will be much easier to search on the surname field.

DESIGNING THE DATABASE

When you think of the structure of the database you should think of what the table will look like without any information in it at all (the design of the table). To describe the structure you need to know some things:

The number of fields (columns) in the table

The field names (column headings)

The data type of each field

The number of rows will increase as we enter more.

It is important to know the difference between the database structure (think of it as empty with no records) and the data entered into the database (the information that you put on the table).

For each of the following changes to the Database bellow, would you need to change the database structure or edit the database?

Question 1 You decide to add a new field name ContactInfo, to the database.

Question 2 Bob Harris is actually from Paris.

Customer Name	Date of birth	Location
Bob Harris	01/03/2001	London
Mary Reynolds	17/01/2002	London
Mark Smith	28/09/2000	New York
Lily Grant	21/06/2000	Madrid

Answer 1 If you add a new field name, you are changing the database structure

Answer 2 If you are changing the record for Bob Harris you are only editing the data.

NAMING CONVENTIONS

We will use a common name format when creating names for tables and field names. This means putting tbl in front of the table names, and not using spaces in between words. Use capital letters in the middle of a field name to make the words easier to read. Look at the table below to see an example.

Information about the database structure can be shown in a table, like this one:

tblMember

Field name	Data Type
PupilNo	AutoNumber
FirstName	Text
Surname	Text

ContactName	Text
ContactNo	Text
DateOfBirth	Date/Time
Activity	Text
Amount Paid	Currency
Transport?	Y/N

This will be the database structure of the SchoolTripDatabase.

Chapter 2

CREATING A NEW DATABASE

Over the next several chapters you'll be creating and developing the Activities database.

LOADING ACCESS

You can load Access in one of two ways:

- Either double click the Access icon on the main screen in Windows

- Or click the Start button at the bottom left of the screen, then click Programs, then click Microsoft Access 2010.

 Microsoft Access 2010

Your screen will look like this;

You now have the option of either opening an existing database or creating a new one. We will create a new database from scratch.

- Select Blank Database button.

- Click on the Create New Folder button and create a new folder named YouthClub.

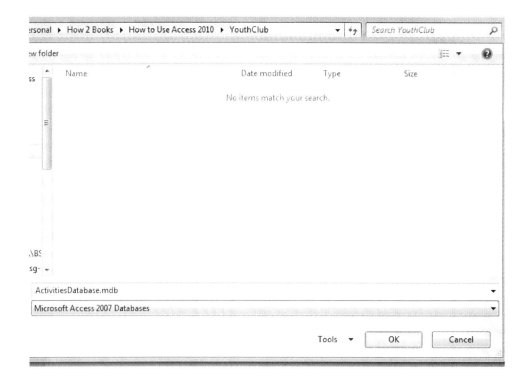

- In the File Name box, type the name ActivitesDatabase (no spaces).

- Click OK and press the Create button. Access will automatically add the file extension .mdb.

THE DATABASE STRUCTURE

The first thing you have to do is to set up the database structure. As you learnt in the first chapter, all the data in an Access database is stored in tables. A table has a row for each record and a column for each field. The first thing you have to do is tell Access exactly what data type each field is. After this has been done and the structure is saved, you can start adding data to the database.

THE DATABASE WINDOW

Access database are made up of objects. A table is an object, and is the only objects we have talked about so far. Other objects which you will come across in this book include Queries, Forms and Reports.

CREATING A NEW TABLE

- Click on the create tab.

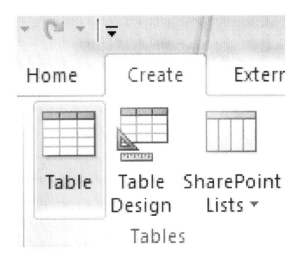

- Select table. You will see this table

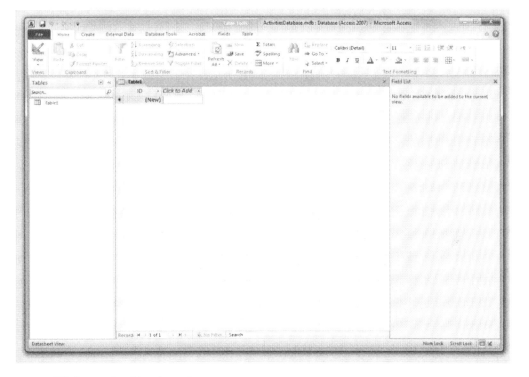

- Click on the Home tab.

Every Access Database has a Database window. This is like a central menu for your database, from which you can open the objects in your database. The window has tabs for each type of database object (Tables, Queries, Forms, Reports, etc).

- In the database menu on the left make sure the tables option is selected.

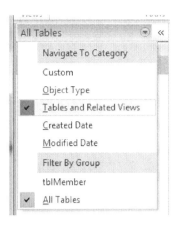

- Click on View and select Design View from the drop down menu.

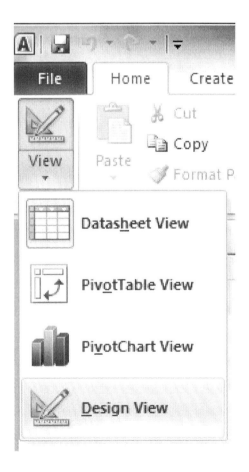

- At this point you must give the table and name. Enter the name tblPupil and click OK.

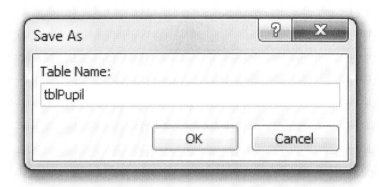

Look back at the structure of the table. All the fields need to be entered into the new table.

- Enter the first field name, PupilNo, and press tab to highlight the Data Type column.

- Click the Down arrow and select the field type AutoNumber.
- Press tab to the Description column and type. This is the Key field.

tblPupil		
Field Name	Data Type	Description
PupilNo	AutoNumber	This is the key field

DEFINING THE PRIMARY KEY

Every table in an Access database must have a primary key (also known as the key field). The field which is your primary key must be different for each record. For our Activities database we will set PupilNo to be the primary key. We cannot use FirstName because there may be more than one member with the same first name.

- Right click in the row for MemberNo, select the Primary Key icon. The key symbol will appear in the left hand margin next to MemberNo.

	Field Name	Data Type	
PupilNo		AutoNumber	This is the key field

Primary Key

ENTERING ANOTHER FIELD

- Now we can enter all the other fields.
- In the next row, enter the field name FirstName and leave the data type in the next column as Text.
- Enter the fields for Surname, ContactName and ContactNo. All these fields have a data type Text.

- Enter the field name DateOfBirth and give it a data type of Date/Time.

- Enter the field name Activity and leave the data type as Text.

- Enter the field name Amount Paid and give it the data type Currency.

- Enter the field name Transport? And give it a data type Yes/No.

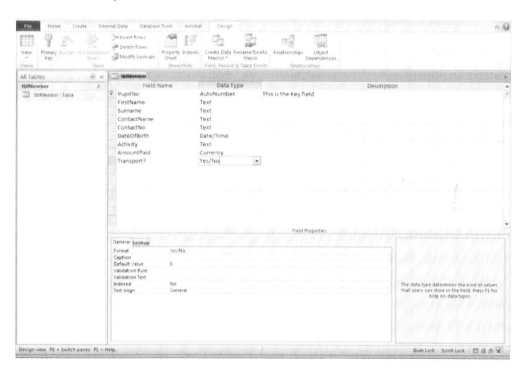

SAVING THE TABLE STRUCTURE

- Save the updates you have made to the structure by pressing the Save button or selecting the File tab, Click on Save.

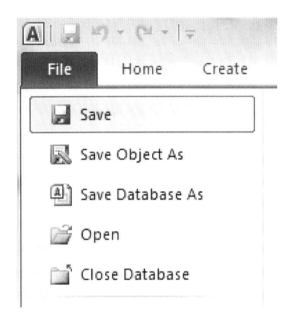

- If you are asked to type a name for your table. Type the name tblMember and click OK.
- Click on the close button on the top right of the table

EDITING A TABLE STRUCTURE

Look to see the list of all tables on the left of your screen. Under this you will see a list of the tables in your database. In our case you will just see the new table.

- Double click on tblMember.
- Click on View to show the different views available, select Design view.

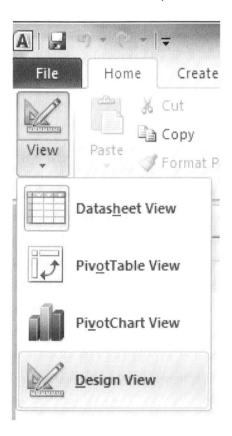

INSERTING A FIELD

Look and see the list of all tables on the left of your screen. Under this you will see a list of the tables in your database. In our case you will just see the new table.

- Double click on tblPupil.

- Click on View to show the different views available, select Design view.

To insert another field you will insert a new row. In our case we will add an emergency number (maybe a work or mobile number.) Just above DateOfBirth:

- Click on the row selector for DateOfBirth.

- Click on the Insert Rows Button or Press Insert on your keyboard.

- Enter the new Field EmergencyNumber, data type Text.

Field Name	Data Type	
PupilNo	AutoNumber	This
FirstName	Text	
Surname	Text	
ContactName	Text	
ContactNo	Text	
EmergencyNumber	Text	
DateOfBirth	Date/Time	
Activity	Text	
AmountPaid	Currency	
Transport?	Yes/No	

DELETING A FIELD

- Delete the field you have just inserted;

- Select the field by clicking the row selector for EmergencyNumber

- Press the Delete Rows button or the delete key.

MOVING A FIELD

Click the row selector that you want to move and then click and hold the left mouse button again in the box to the left of the highlighted row.

You will be able to drag the field to where you want.

- Try to move the Activity field down to be between the below the Amount Paid field.

The black line will show you where it will move.

tblPupil		
Field Name	Data Type	
PupilNo	AutoNumber	This is the key field
FirstName	Text	
Surname	Text	
ContactName	Text	
ContactNo	Text	
DateOfBirth	Date/Time	
Activity	Text	
AmountPaid	Currency	
Transport?	Yes/No	

CHANGING OR REMOVING A FIELD

- To change the key field to be Surname, click the row selector for Surname and then click on the Primary key button

tblPupil		
Field Name	Data Type	
PupilNo	AutoNumber	This is the key field
FirstName	Text	
Surname	Text	
ContactName	Text	

- To remove the key field completely, press the Primary key button again.

tblPupil		
Field Name	Data Type	
PupilNo	AutoNumber	This is the key field
FirstName	Text	
Surname	Text	
ContactName	Text	

Before we continue to the next Chapter….

- Restore you database and make the PupilNo the Primary Key.

tblPupil		
Field Name	Data Type	
⑧▶ PupilNo	AutoNumber	This is the key field
FirstName	Text	

- Save and Close the Database from the Microsoft Office button.

If you are prompted too, save any changes you want to keep.

Chapter 3

OPENING AN EXISTING DATABASE

- Open access.

Your screen will look like this;

From here you should see the window the first appeared when you open Access 2010 the first time around. However now you will be able to see recently opened database files on the right (inc your database).

- Double click on SchoolTripDatabase to open your file.

You will now see this window.

TABLE VIEWS

There are two views we will be using to make changes to our database;

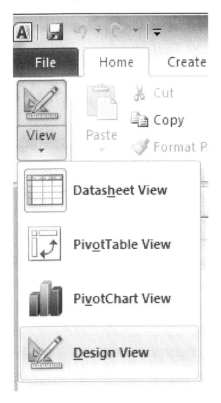

Design View – Is used to change the structure of the database e.g. adding fields or changing fields' names or data types

Datasheet View – Is used to enter and editing the data.

ENTERING DATA

Double click on tblPupil. Tip; if you cannot see the table, select the drop down box where you can see "All Tables" to select Tables and Related Views.

You should see the Pupils table below.

You can drag the right border of any column header/ field name to alter its width.

- If you move your cursor on top of the line in-between the field names your cursor will change shape.

- Now drag the borders so that the whole of the names appear on the screen.

- Click on the First row of the PupilNo where it says (New).

You do not need to enter anything here as it is an AutoNumber data type and Access will automatically enter a number here for you.

- Click on the next box to the right.

- Type Sarah

- Go to Surname and enter Reynolds

- Go to ContactName and type Mr Reynolds

- Go to ContactNo and type 01355 480480

- Go to DateOfBirth and type 28/06/2000

- Enter Cook and Create

- Leave amount paid as 0.00

You will not need to enter the £, $ or € sign as we have made it a Currency data type. Access will use your computers local settings to pick the currency.

- In the Transport? Field, tick the box.

You should see the same as the table below:

Don't worry about the number that is created automatically in the column for the PupilNo. Now enter the data from the table below;

FirstName	Surname	ContactName	ContactNo	DateOfBirth	Activity	AmountPaid	Transport?
Paul	Smith	Mr Smith	01356667800	01/04/1999	Cook and Create	50	Y
Natasha	Baker	Mrs Baker	01355450900	13/03/2001	Cowboy Adventure	25	N
William	Khan	Mrs Khan	01355607010	21/09/2000	Mountain Biking	50	N
Wendy	Mason	Mr Larson	01355499090	26/01/1999	Cowboy Adventure	50	Y

| Callum | Wilson | Mr Wilson | 01355322130 | 29/11/2001 | Mountain Biking | 25 | Y |
| Kerry | Conn | Mrs Conn | 01355336640 | 08/01/2000 | Mountain Biking | 50 | Y |

It should look like this;

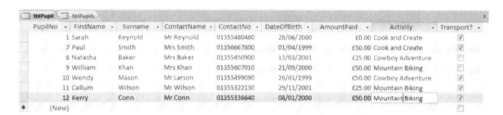

As you can see my number vary from 1 -12, don't worry if your numbers are different.

When you have entered all the data from the table, click on the close button on the top right of the table.

- You may be asked to save the changes you have made.

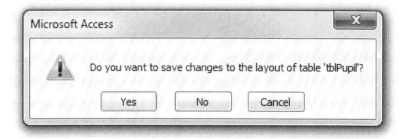

- Click on Yes and you will be at the same window as you were at the start of the chapter.

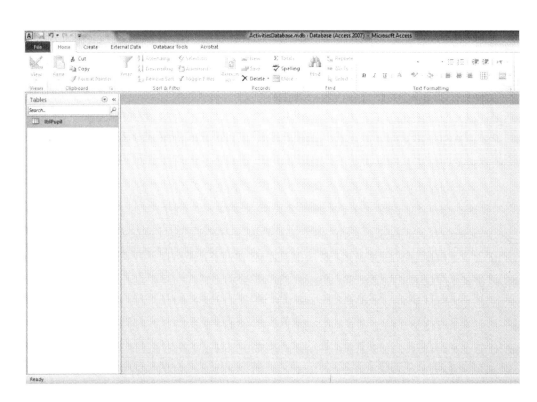

FINDING, EDITING AND DELETING DATA IN A

TABLE

Make sure the table is selected on the left menu. You are going to open the tblPupil again.

- Double click on tblPupil.

This will open the table in datasheet view and it should look like this.

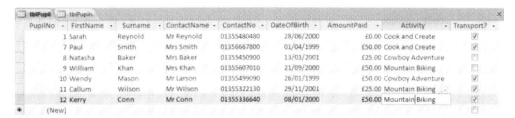

PupilNo	FirstName	Surname	ContactName	ContactNo	DateOfBirth	AmountPaid	Activity	Transport?
1	Sarah	Reynold	Mr Reynold	01355480480	28/06/2000	£0.00	Cook and Create	✓
7	Paul	Smith	Mrs Smith	01356667800	01/04/1999	£50.00	Cook and Create	✓
8	Natasha	Baker	Mrs Baker	01355450900	13/03/2001	£25.00	Cowboy Adventure	
9	William	Khan	Mrs Khan	01355607010	21/09/2000	£50.00	Mountain Biking	
10	Wendy	Mason	Mr Larson	01355499090	26/01/1999	£50.00	Cowboy Adventure	✓
11	Callum	Wilson	Mr Wilson	01355322130	29/11/2001	£25.00	Mountain Biking	✓
12	Kerry	Conn	Mr Conn	01355336640	08/01/2000	£50.00	Mountain Biking	✓
	(New)							

USING THE RECORD SELECTORS

In a real database they will have large tables with hundreds of records. You might want to find one person or information in the datasheet view. Using this section at the bottom of the table you can go to the first, last or add a new record.

Record: I◀ ◀ 1 of 7 ▶ ▶I ▶❇ 🗙 No Filter | Search

FINDING A RECORD

If you want to find a particular record you will use the find icon. This will be really useful on a larger database with lots of records.

Find

- Click the mouse anywhere in the Surname column, except in Wendy Masson's record.

We are going to find the record for Wendy Mason.

- Click on the find button on the main toolbar/Ribbon.

- Type Mason next to Find What?

- Press enter or click on find next

Wendy's record should now be highlighted

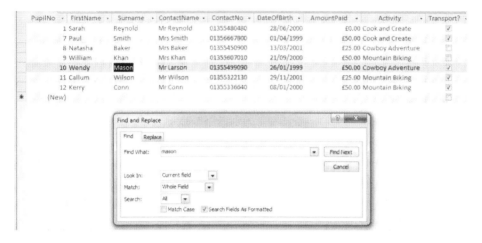

- Close Find and replace window by clicking it Close icon

EDITING DATA

You can change any of the data in the table, apart from PupilNo as it is an AutoNumber field.

To edit a field you can click in the field and editing by using the Backspace or Delete key to remove the contents and type in the correction.

Remember you can use the undo button if you make a mistake!

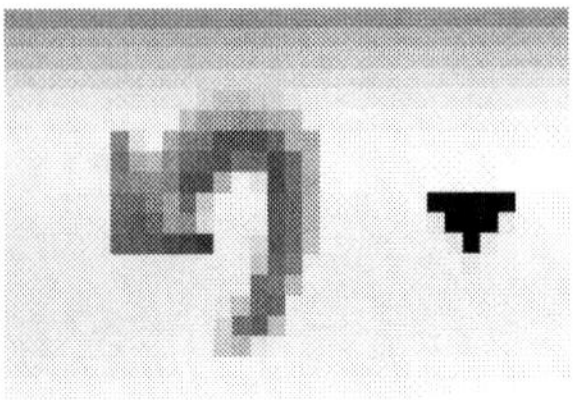

ADDING A NEW RECORD

A new Pupil has joined the trip and has given their details in the table below;

First Name	Surname	Contact Name	Contact No	Date Of Birth	Amount Paid	Activity	Transport
Amy	Bond	Mr Bond	01325 709007	12/12/2001	£0	Cowboy Adventures	Yes

There are **two** ways to enter a new record;

The first way is the easiest way for small databases like ours, but if we were using a database with hundreds or thousands of records you would find it easier to use the New Record button.

1st Way – Using the Blank line

- Click on the Blank line next to (New)

PupilNo	FirstName	Surname	ContactName	ContactNo	DateOfBirth	AmountPaid	Activity	Transport?
1 Sarah		Reynold	Mr Reynold	01355480480	28/06/2000	£0.00	Cook and Create	✓
7 Paul		Smith	Mrs Smith	01356667800	01/04/1999	£50.00	Cook and Create	✓
8 Natasha		Baker	Mrs Baker	01355450900	13/03/2001	£25.00	Cowboy Adventure	
9 William		Khan	Mrs Khan	01355607010	21/09/2000	£50.00	Mountain Biking	
10 Wendy		Mason	Mr Larson	01355499090	26/01/1999	£50.00	Cowboy Adventure	✓
11 Callum		Wilson	Mr Wilson	01355322130	29/11/2001	£25.00	Mountain Biking	✓
12 Kerry		Conn	Mr Conn	01355336640	08/01/2000	£50.00	Mountain Biking	✓
(New)								

2nd Way - New Record Button

Press the New Record Button, which is at the bottom of the table frame. It is the furthest arrow to the right

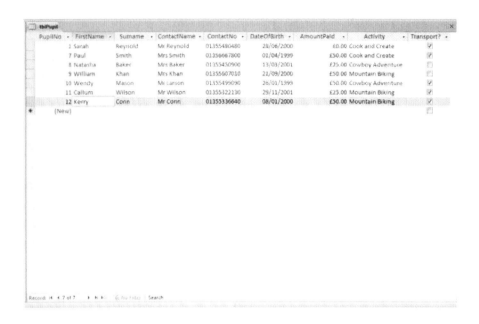

You will find the new record button here;

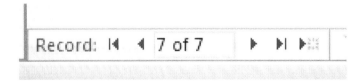

Now using either way;

- Type in Amy's details from the previous table.

DELETING A RECORD

You may need to delete a record from your database. We are going to delete William's record as he is no longer going.

- Click anywhere in William's record

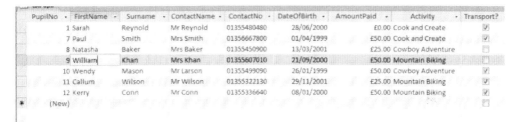

- Select the Delete menu, by clicking on the arrow next to delete.

- Select Delete Record.

You will get a warning like this which you have to approve before it is deleted.

- Click on Yes, You can see that the record for William has been deleted.

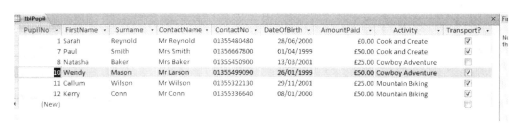

Chapter 4

It is important the information you add to a database in correct as mistakes can be hard to spot in a very large database. For example if you entered "Mountain Bike" instead of "Mountain Biking" as an activity for a pupil, when you search for all those pupils doing that "Mountain Biking" that pupil would not be shown.

i   Some mistakes cannot be prevented in a database, such as misspelt names. But Database software can help to prevent lots of others.

You can create a rule in a database. That means if anyone entered new information or edits old information, the information must match the rule, for example;

i All date of birth fields must be within a sensible range for pupils on the trip.

i Only Cook and Create, Cowboy Adventure and Mountain Biking can be entered in the Activity field.

i The value of AmountPaid cannot be more than a certain limit. If you know the maximum cost to be £20, you can set that as the limit.

WHAT HAPPENS IF?

What happens if the information you have entered, doesn't not match the rule? You can make text to appear in a warning to show the person adding new information that they have entered invalid information. This is called Validation Text.

TYPES OF RULE

There are lots of different types of rules you can enter, Look at the table below to see them.

Symbol	Meaning	Example
<	Less than	<10
<=	Less than or equal to	<=10
>	Greater than	>1
>=	Greater than or equal to	>=1
=	Equal to	=5 ="Mountain Biking"
<>	Not equal to	<>"Mountain Biking"
BETWEEN	Test for a range between two values	BETWEEN 13/01/2001 AND 13/02/2001

ENTERING THE VALIDATION RULES

- Open the File SchoolTripDatabase

- In the database window makes sure the "Tables" view is ticked.

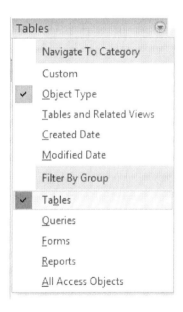

- Double click on tblPupil

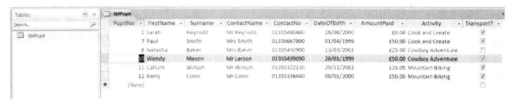

- Click on View

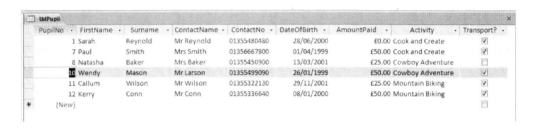

- Select Design View

You are going to enter a validation rule for the DateOfBirth field. The rule that you will use is; DateOfBirth must be between 01/01/1999 and 01/01/2002.

You should see something like this;

Field Name	Data Type	
tblPupil		
PupilNo	AutoNumber	This is the key field
FirstName	Text	
Surname	Text	
ContactName	Text	
ContactNo	Text	
DateOfBirth	Date/Time	
AmountPaid	Currency	
Activity	Text	
Transport?	Yes/No	

General Lookup

Field Size	Long Integer
New Values	Increment
Format	
Caption	
Indexed	Yes (No Duplicates)
Smart Tags	
Text Align	General

Help.

- Click in the FirstName Field.

tblPupil		
Field Name	**Data Type**	
PupilNo	AutoNumber	This is the ke'
FirstName|	Text	
Surname	Text	
ContactName	Text	
ContactNo	Text	
DateOfBirth	Date/Time	
AmountPaid	Currency	
Activity	Text	
Transport?	Yes/No	

Notice that there are two rows in the Field Properties area of the window.

One is called Validation Rule and one is called Validation Text.

General	Lookup	
Field Size	255
Format	
Input Mask	
Caption	
Default Value	
Validation Rule	
Validation Text	
Required	No
Allow Zero Length	Yes
Indexed	No
Unicode Compression	Yes
IME Mode	No Control
IME Sentence Mode	None
Smart Tags	

This is where we will enter the rules.

- Click on the DateOfBirth field name.

- In the Field Properties, click in the Validation Rule row

tblPupil		
Field Name	Data Type	
PupilNo	AutoNumber	This
FirstName	Text	
Surname	Text	
ContactName	Text	
ContactNo	Text	
DateOfBirth	Date/Time	
AmountPaid	Currency	
Activity	Text	
Transport?	Yes/No	

General | Lookup

Format	
Input Mask	
Caption	
Default Value	
Validation Rule	
Validation Text	
Required	No
Indexed	No
IME Mode	No Control
IME Sentence Mode	None
Smart Tags	
Text Align	General
Show Date Picker	For dates

- Type exactly "Between 01/01/1999 And 01/01/2002".

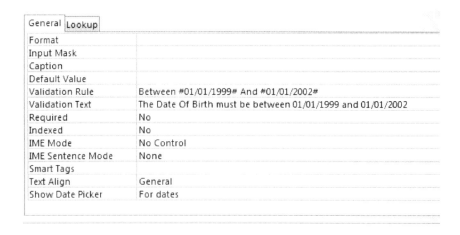

General	Lookup	
Format		
Input Mask		
Caption		
Default Value		
Validation Rule	Between #01/01/1999# And #01/01/2002#	
Validation Text		
Required	No	
Indexed	No	
IME Mode	No Control	
IME Sentence Mode	None	
Smart Tags		
Text Align	General	
Show Date Picker	For dates	

Notice how Access has put a # sign either side of the date

- Press Enter

- Click in the Validation Text row

- Type exactly "The Date Of Birth must be between 01/01/1999 and 01/01/2002".

Press Enter. It should now look like this;

General	Lookup	
Format		
Input Mask		
Caption		
Default Value		
Validation Rule	Between #01/01/1999# And #01/01/2002#	
Validation Text	The Date Of Birth must be between 01/01/1999 and 01/01/2002	
Required	No	
Indexed	No	
IME Mode	No Control	
IME Sentence Mode	None	
Smart Tags		
Text Align	General	
Show Date Picker	For dates	

We are going to return to Datasheet View

- Click on View and Click on Datasheet View.

You will be asked to save the changes you have just made.

- Click on Yes

- Click on Yes when access asks about the data integrity rules to check the information you have already entered matches the new rule.

TIME TO TEST THE RULE

We will test the rule by entering a new record that we know will not work.

- Click on the blank row to enter a new record.

- Enter the FirstName as Emily

- Enter the Surname, ContactName and ContactNo for Emily as shown in the table above.

First Name	Surname	Contact Name	Contact No	Date Of Birth	Amount Paid	Activity	Transport
Emily	Holden	Mr Bentley	01325 204401	1/08/98	£20	Cowboy Adventure	Yes

- Enter the DateOfBirth as 01/08/98 and Press Enter.

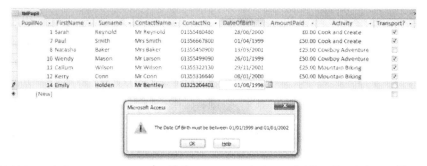

At this point as you can asks if the person is too old for the trip or if the DateOfBirth is wrong.

- Click on OK.

- Change the DateOfBirth to 01/08/99

- Enter the rest of the details for Emily.

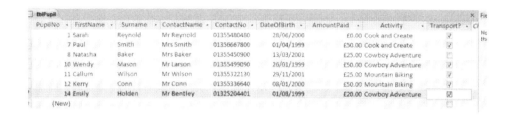

PupilNo	FirstName	Surname	ContactName	ContactNo	DateOfBirth	AmountPaid	Activity	Transport?	Cl
1 Sarah	Reynold	Mr Reynold	01355480480	28/06/2000	£0.00	Cook and Create	✓	Nc thi
7 Paul	Smith	Mrs Smith	01356667800	01/04/1999	£50.00	Cook and Create	✓	
8 Natasha	Baker	Mrs Baker	01355450900	13/03/2001	£25.00	Cowboy Adventure	☐	
10 Wendy	Mason	Mr Larson	01355499090	26/01/1999	£50.00	Cowboy Adventure	✓	
11 Callum	Wilson	Mr Wilson	01355322130	29/11/2001	£25.00	Mountain Biking	✓	
12 Kerry	Conn	Mr Conn	01355336640	08/01/2000	£50.00	Mountain Biking	✓	
14 Emily	Holden	Mr Bentley	01325204401	01/08/1999	£20.00	Cowboy Adventure	☑	
(New)								☐	

SETTING THE OTHER VALIDATION RULES

Now we are going to set the rule for the Activity field. The rule will be to only allow Cook and Create, Cowboy Adventure or Mountain Biking.

- Go back to design View by clicking on View and Selecting the Design View Button.

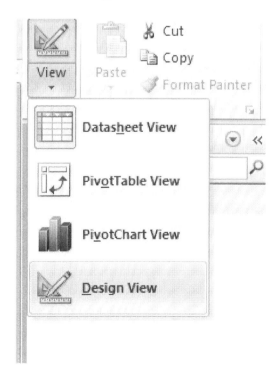

- Click in the field name for Activity, to shows its field properties.

Field Name	Data Type	
PupilNo	AutoNumber	This is the key fi
FirstName	Text	
Surname	Text	
ContactName	Text	
ContactNo	Text	
DateOfBirth	Date/Time	
AmountPaid	Currency	
Activity	Text	
Transport?	Yes/No	

tblPupil

General Lookup

Field Size	255
Format	
Input Mask	
Caption	
Default Value	
Validation Rule	
Validation Text	
Required	No
Allow Zero Length	Yes
Indexed	No
Unicode Compression	Yes
IME Mode	No Control
IME Sentence Mode	None
Smart Tags	

- Click in the Validation Rule row of the field properties

- Type exactly ="Cook and Create" or "Cowboy Adventure" or "Mountain Biking"

General	Lookup
Field Size	255
Format	
Input Mask	
Caption	
Default Value	
Validation Rule	="Cook and Create" Or "Cowboy Adventure" Or "Mountain Biking"
Validation Text	
Required	No
Allow Zero Length	Yes
Indexed	No
Unicode Compression	Yes
IME Mode	No Control
IME Sentence Mode	None
Smart Tags	

- Press Enter

- Click in the Validation Text row.

- Type Exactly Enter Cook and Create, Cowboy Adventure or Mountain Biking.

General	Lookup
Field Size	255
Format	
Input Mask	
Caption	
Default Value	
Validation Rule	="Cook and Create" Or "Cowboy Adventure" Or "Mountain Biking"
Validation Text	Enter Cook and Create, Cowboy Adventure or Mountain Biking
Required	No
Allow Zero Length	Yes
Indexed	No
Unicode Compression	Yes
IME Mode	No Control
IME Sentence Mode	None
Smart Tags	

- Press Enter

- We are going to enter the rule for the AmountPaid

- Click in the field row for Amount Paid

- Enter the Validation text "AmountPaid cannot exceed £50"

- Enter the Validation Rule <=50

- Press Enter

This is what it should look like.

General	Lookup	
Format	Currency
Decimal Places	Auto
Input Mask	
Caption	
Default Value	
Validation Rule	< = 50
Validation Text	AmountPaid cannot exceed £50
Required	No
Indexed	Yes (Duplicates OK)
Smart Tags	
Text Align	General

TIME TO TEST AGAIN

- Go to the Datasheet View
- Click on Yes to save the changes and

- Click on Yes to any prompt about the data integrity just like before.

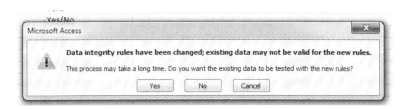

It is always good to Test your validation rules by entering invalid information. You can delete any record to cancel the test record.

- Try Entering the following records containing invalid values.

  You should see your error message appear.

First Name	Surname	Contact Name	Contact No	Date Of Birth	Amount Paid	Activity	Transport
Sunil	Basu	Mrs Basu	01325 268901	29/08/1199	£10	Cowboy Adventure	Yes
James	Appleton	Mrs Appleton	01322 334455	21/08/2000	£55	Cook and Create	No
Sarah	Jenkins	Mrs Jenkins	01331 664499	03//03/2001	£0	Mountains Biking	Yes

- Correct the obvious mistakes to your database, so that your table looks like this.

12 Kerry	Conn	Mr Conn	01355336640	08/01/2000	£50.00 Mountain Biking	☒
14 Emily	Holden	Mr Bentley	01325204401	01/08/1999	£20.00 Cowboy Adventure	☑
15 Sunil	Basu	Mrs Basu	01325268901	29/08/1999	£10.00 Cowboy Adventure	☑
16 James	Appleton	Mrs Appleton	01322334455	21/08/2000	£25.00 Cook and Create	☐
17 Sarah	Jenkins	Mrs Jenkins	01331664499	03/03/2001	£0.00 Mountain Biking	☑

- Save and Close your Database.

- Close Access.

Chapter 5

- Open the file SchoolTripDatabase
- Double Click on tblPupil : Table

SORTING RECORDS

To sort the Pupils in the table by their surname;

- Click in the Surname Field

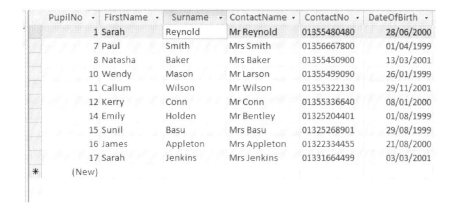

PupilNo ▾	FirstName ▾	Surname ▾	ContactName ▾	ContactNo ▾	DateOfBirth ▾
1	Sarah	Reynold	Mr Reynold	01355480480	28/06/2000
7	Paul	Smith	Mrs Smith	01356667800	01/04/1999
8	Natasha	Baker	Mrs Baker	01355450900	13/03/2001
10	Wendy	Mason	Mr Larson	01355499090	26/01/1999
11	Callum	Wilson	Mr Wilson	01355322130	29/11/2001
12	Kerry	Conn	Mr Conn	01355336640	08/01/2000
14	Emily	Holden	Mr Bentley	01325204401	01/08/1999
15	Sunil	Basu	Mrs Basu	01325268901	29/08/1999
16	James	Appleton	Mrs Appleton	01322334455	21/08/2000
17	Sarah	Jenkins	Mrs Jenkins	01331664499	03/03/2001
*	(New)				

- Press the Sort Ascending Button.

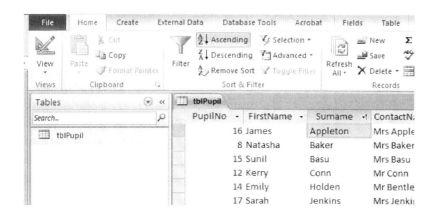

Now you will see the records ordered from A to Z by

the Surname field.

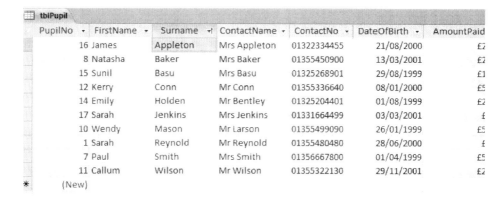

You will be able to see a sort icon at the top of the surname
column to show the table has been sorted by this field.

FORMATTING AND PRINTING A DATASHEET

- With tblPupil open in Datasheet View

- Click on the File tab

- Click on Print and Print Preview.

You will see that the whole datasheet will not fit on one page

in Portrait view. You can use the page Selector at the bottom of the

window to view to second page.

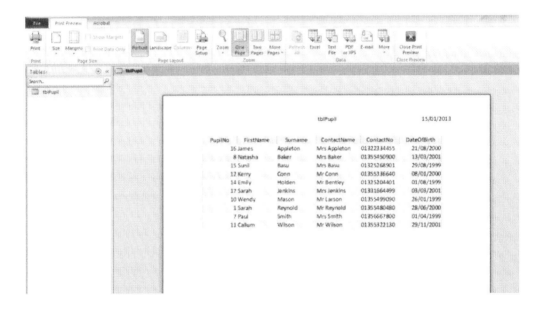

tblPupil   15/01/2013

PupilNo	FirstName	Surname	ContactName	ContactNo	DateOfBirth
16	James	Appleton	Mrs Appleton	01322334455	21/08/2000
8	Natasha	Baker	Mrs Baker	01355450900	13/03/2001
15	Sunil	Basu	Mrs Basu	01325268901	29/08/1999
12	Kerry	Conn	Mr Conn	01355336640	08/01/2000
14	Emily	Holden	Mr Bentley	01325204401	01/08/1999
17	Sarah	Jenkins	Mrs Jenkins	01331664499	03/03/2001
10	Wendy	Mason	Mr Larson	01355499090	26/01/1999
1	Sarah	Reynold	Mr Reynold	01355480480	28/06/2000
7	Paul	Smith	Mrs Smith	01356667800	01/04/1999
11	Callum	Wilson	Mr Wilson	01355322130	29/11/2001

- Click on the right arrow

You will now see page 2 with the rest of the datasheet view.

tblPupil

AmountPaid	Activity	Transport?
£25.00	Cook and Create	☐
£25.00	Cowboy Adventure	☐
£10.00	Cowboy Adventure	☑
£50.00	Mountain Biking	☑
£20.00	Cowboy Adventure	☑
£0.00	Mountain Biking	☑
£50.00	Cowboy Adventure	☑
£0.00	Cook and Create	☑
£50.00	Cook and Create	☑
£25.00	Mountain Biking	☑

Look at the Print Preview toolbar at the top of the window. You can see other features to preview your datasheet.

You can Zoom in on a page and Zoom out. View One or Two pages at the same time.

- Click on the Landscape button to see if the Datasheet will fit onto one page.

It should now fit. Let's now return to the Datasheet View.

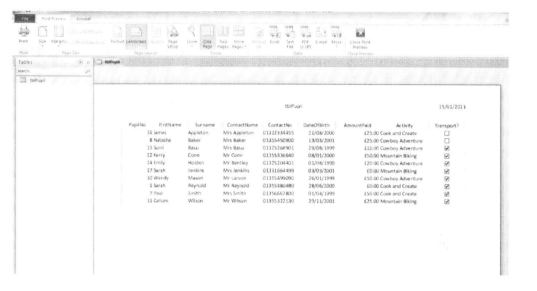

- Click on Close Print Preview

Close Print
Preview
Close Preview

HIDING AND UNHIDING COLUMNS

Sometimes you may not want to print all the columns in the datasheet. You can hide the columns you don't want to see.

- Make sure you have tblPupil open in Datasheet View

PupilNo	FirstName	Surname	ContactName	ContactNo	DateOfBirth	AmountPaid	Activity	Transport?
16	James	Appleton	Mrs Appleton	01322334455	21/08/2000	£25.00	Cook and Create	☐
8	Natasha	Baker	Mrs Baker	01355450900	13/03/2001	£25.00	Cowboy Adventure	☐
15	Sunil	Basu	Mrs Basu	01325268901	29/08/1999	£10.00	Cowboy Adventure	☑
12	Kerry	Conn	Mr Conn	01355336640	08/01/2000	£50.00	Mountain Biking	☑
14	Emily	Holden	Mr Bentley	01325204401	01/08/1999	£20.00	Cowboy Adventure	☑
17	Sarah	Jenkins	Mrs Jenkins	01331664499	03/03/2001	£0.00	Mountain Biking	☑
10	Wendy	Mason	Mr Larson	01355499090	26/01/1999	£50.00	Cowboy Adventure	☑
1	Sarah	Reynold	Mr Reynold	01355480480	28/06/2000	£0.00	Cook and Create	☑
7	Paul	Smith	Mrs Smith	01356667800	01/04/1999	£50.00	Cook and Create	☑
11	Callum	Wilson	Mr Wilson	01355322130	29/11/2001	£25.00	Mountain Biking	☑
(New)								☐

- Drag across the column headers / field

  names AmountPaid, Activity and Transport?

- Right click

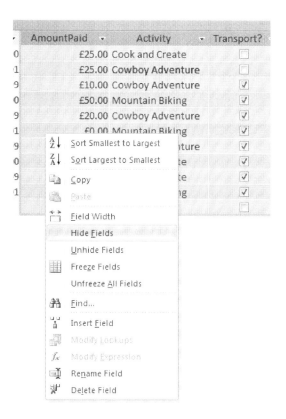

- Select Hide Columns

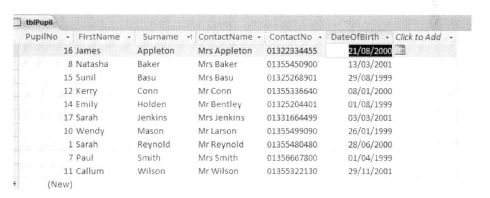

The columns are now hidden to be printed if you wanted. To get them back;

- Right click on one of the field names / column headers

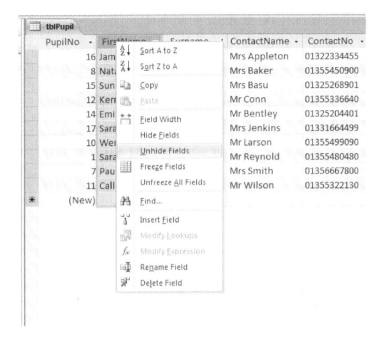

- Select Unhide columns

You will not see this window to select the fields you want to see.

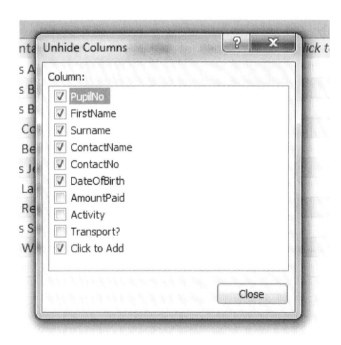

- Tick all the Columns

- Click on Close

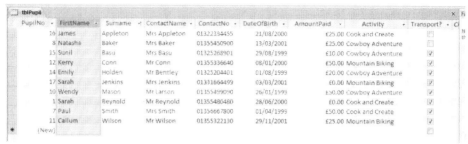

You will now see the columns are now not hidden anymore.

FORMATTING COLUMNS

Suppose you wanted to move DateOfBirth column to the end.

- Click the DateOfBirth column Header.
- Click again and hold down the mouse button, then drag the header to the right end of the table.
- Adjust the column widths by double clicking in the column heard on the border between each column

Your table should now look like this

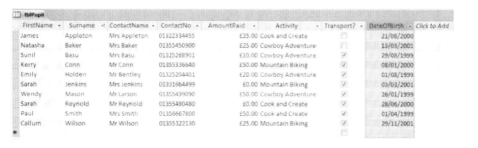

- Click on the Print preview menu to see what the page will look like when printed out now.

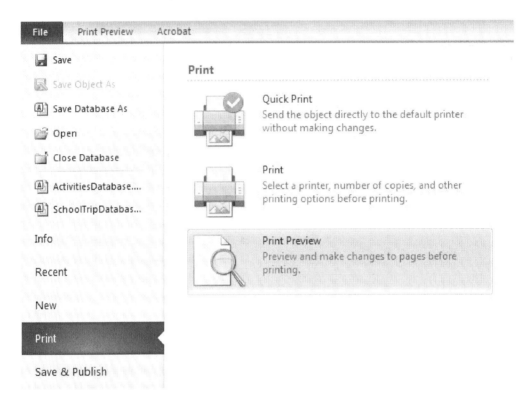

- Click on Close and click Yes if prompted to save and changes.

Chapter 6

MAKING QUERIES

One of the most useful things databases allow you to do is to search

of records that only contain one condition, such as, all those going

Mountain Biking. This is where you query your database.

Open Access and open the SchoolTripDatabase.

CREATING A NEW QUERY

- Click on the Create tab at the top of the window.

You will now see a different ribbon. Like this;

- Click on Query Design.

You will see a window Asking which table to show in the query, you will see your tblPupil

- Click on tblPupil and click Add
- Click on Close to close the Window

You will now see you table field names has been added.

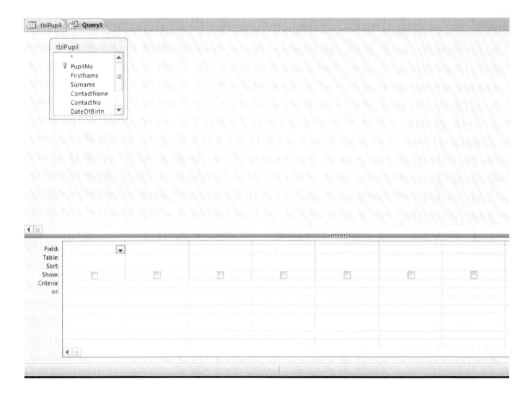

SELECTING THE FIELDS TO APPEAR IN THE QUERY

A query grid will appear, you will need to select the fields on the grid from the tblPupil table. These will be the fields for which you want to specify condition, called criteria.

- In the upper pane of the window double click on the fields FirstName, Surname, DateOfBirth and Acitvity.

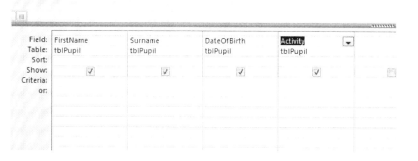

You will see the fields added on the query grid. You could also use the Drop down menu.

Suppose you now wanted to delete the DateOfBirth fields from the query.

- Click in the column header of the DateOfBirth field to select the column and press the Delete key.

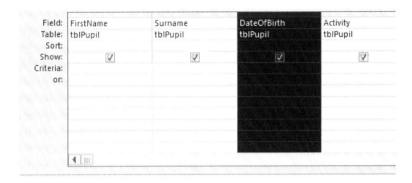

- Click in the Empty field row to the right of Activity and use the drop down menu to select Transport?

- Now make sure tick the row in the Show row is selected.

SETTING SIMPLE CRITERIA

Now suppose you want to find all the members who have chosen Cook and Create as their activity.

- In the criteria row of the Activity column, enter "Cook and Create"

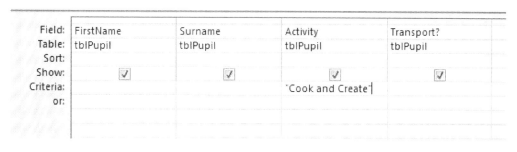

Field:	FirstName	Surname	Activity	Transport?
Table:	tblPupil	tblPupil	tblPupil	tblPupil
Sort:				
Show:	✓	✓	✓	✓
Criteria:			"Cook and Create"	
or:				

Run

- Now press Run on the ribbon.

You will now see the results;

FirstName ▾	Surname ▾	Activity ▾	Transport? ▾
Paul	Smith	Cook and Create	✓
James	Appleton	Cook and Create	
Sarah	Reynold	Cook and Create	✓
*			

SAVING A QUERY

You can save a query so that you can run it whenever you want in the future. This can be useful if you add more records.

- Click on the Save button in the top left of the screen, to save the query.

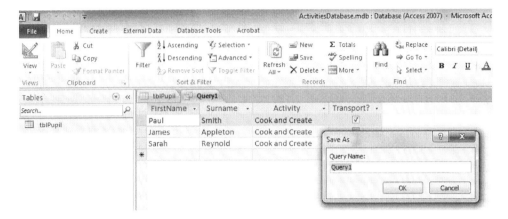

- Save it as qryCookAndCreate, Click OK.

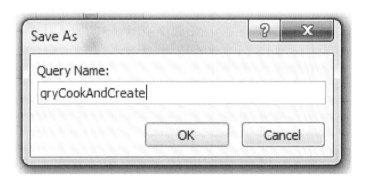

MULTIPLE CRITERIA

Now suppose you wanted to find all the pupils that wanted to do either cook and create or the Cowboy Adventure. Look at the row under Criteria, the heading for this is or.

- Return to Design View to change the query.

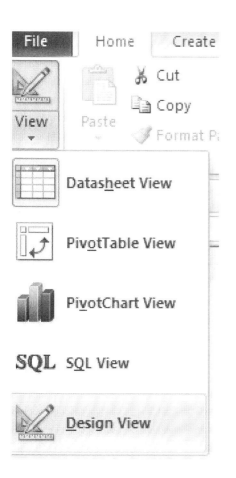

- In the row headed "or", under the criteria "Cook and Create", type "Cowboy Adventure". Like this;

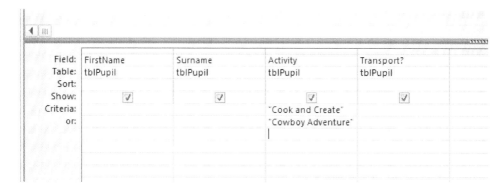

- Run the query again.

Run

Your Results will look like this.

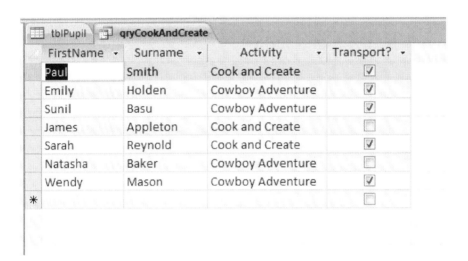

FirstName	Surname	Activity	Transport?
Paul	Smith	Cook and Create	✓
Emily	Holden	Cowboy Adventure	✓
Sunil	Basu	Cowboy Adventure	✓
James	Appleton	Cook and Create	☐
Sarah	Reynold	Cook and Create	✓
Natasha	Baker	Cowboy Adventure	☐
Wendy	Mason	Cowboy Adventure	✓
*			☐

- Click on the Save Object As button

- Save this query as qryCook&Cowboy

- Click on the home tab.

- Right click on the qryCook&Cowboy tab

- Click close.

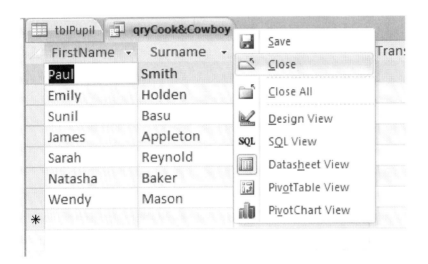

This will close just this query, if you wanted to close all just select Close all to close all your open tabs.

USING COMPARISON OPERATORS

You might need to find records that have data in a field that is less tan or more than something, for example a date of birth or a number. You can use any of the operators we used in Chapter 4 to do this. Here they are again;

Symbol	Meaning	Example
<	Less than	<10
<=	Less than or equal to	<=10
>	Greater than	>1
>=	Greater than or equal to	>=1
=	Equal to	=5 ="Mountain Biking"
<>	Not equal to	<>"Mountain Biking"
BETWEEN	Test for a range between two values	BETWEEN 13/01/2001 AND 13/02/2001

We are going to search for pupils whose dates of birth are between 01/08/1999 and 01/09/2000.

- Open qryCook&Cowboy, by double clicking on it.

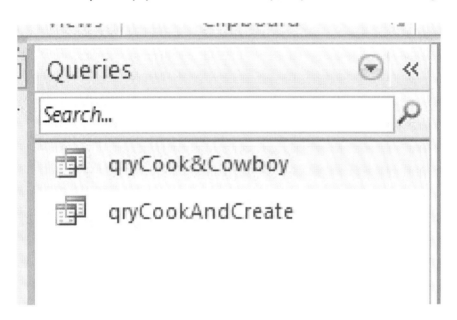

- Change the View to show Design view

- You will see that Access has moved both criteria for our search onto one row.

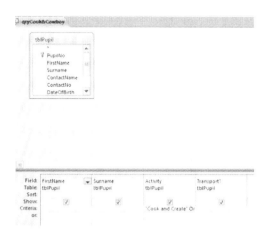

- Drag the Activity Column to make it wider to see all of the criteria.

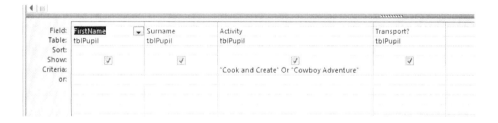

- Add the date of Birth field

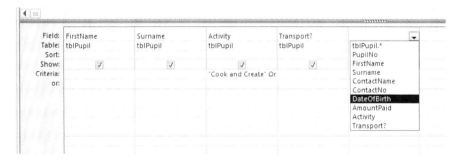

- Type exactly this into the criteria for the DateOfBirth field

Between #01/08/1999# And #01/09/2000#

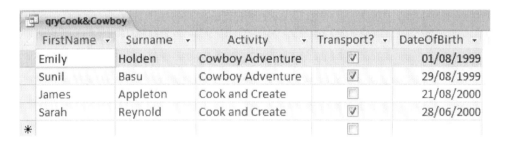

Field:	FirstName	Surname	Activity	Transport?	DateOfBirth
Table:	tblPupil	tblPupil	tblPupil	tblPupil	tblPupil
Sort:					
Show:	✓	✓	✓	✓	✓
Criteria:			"Cook and Create" Or		Between #01/08/1999# And #01/09/2000#
or:					

You might need to make the column wider to see all of the text.

- Click on Run, to run the query. Run

Your results will look like this.

qryCook&Cowboy

FirstName ▾	Surname ▾	Activity ▾	Transport? ▾	DateOfBirth ▾
Emily	Holden	Cowboy Adventure	✓	01/08/1999
Sunil	Basu	Cowboy Adventure	✓	29/08/1999
James	Appleton	Cook and Create	☐	21/08/2000
Sarah	Reynold	Cook and Create	✓	28/06/2000
*			☐	

- Return to design View.

View

Views

SORTING RECORDS

Now we are going to arrange the results to show all the activities together, by sorting the results.

- Click in the Sort row in the Activity column

Field:	FirstName	Surname	Activity		Transport?	DateOfBirth
Table:	tblPupil	tblPupil	tblPupil		tblPupil	tblPupil
Sort:						
Show:	✓	✓	✓	▼	✓	✓
Criteria:			'Cook and Create' Or 'Cowboy Adventure'			Between #01/08/1999# And #01/09/2000#
or:						

- Select Ascending

Field:	FirstName	Surname	Activity		Transport?	DateOfBirth
Table:	tblPupil	tblPupil	tblPupil		tblPupil	tblPupil
Sort:			Ascending	▼		
Show:	✓	✓	✓		✓	✓
Criteria:			'Cook and Create' Or 'Cowboy Adventure'			Between #01/08/1999# And #01/09/2000#
or:						

- Click on Run

Run

Your results will now look like this.

qryCook&Cowboy				
FirstName ▾	Surname ▾	Activity ▾	Transport? ▾	DateOfBirth ▾
Sarah	Reynold	Cook and Create	✓	28/06/2000
James	Appleton	Cook and Create	☐	21/08/2000
Sunil	Basu	Cowboy Adventure	✓	29/08/1999
Emily	Holden	Cowboy Adventure	✓	01/08/1999
*			☐	

This has worked well, but we could improve it. Access has sorted the

Activity column, but the Surnames are not in alphabetical order.

To sort by Activity than by Surname;

View

- Click on design view   Views

- Click on the Surname Field

Field:	FirstName	Surname	Activity	Transport?	DateOfBirth
Table:	tblPupil	tblPupil	tblPupil	tblPupil	tblPupil
Sort:			Ascending		
Show:	✓	✓		✓	✓
Criteria:			"Cook and Create" Or "Cowboy Adventure"		Between #01/08/1999# And #01/09/2000#
or:					

- And in the Sort row, Select Ascending

Field:	FirstName	Surname	Activity	Transport?	DateOfBirth
Table:	tblPupil	tblPupil	tblPupil	tblPupil	tblPupil
Sort:		Ascending	Ascending		
Show:	✓	Ascending		✓	✓
Criteria:		Descending	"Cook and Create" Or "Cowboy Adventure"		Between #01/08/1999# And #01/09/2000#
or:		(not sorted)			

- Now click on run

Run

Your Query results should now look like this.

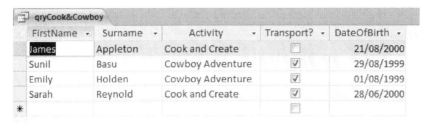

FirstName	Surname	Activity	Transport?	DateOfBirth
James	Appleton	Cook and Create	☐	21/08/2000
Sunil	Basu	Cowboy Adventure	✓	29/08/1999
Emily	Holden	Cowboy Adventure	✓	01/08/1999
Sarah	Reynold	Cook and Create	✓	28/06/2000
*			☐	

qryCook&Cowboy

This is what we want as Access is automatically sorting by Surname before Activity. By default Access uses the column order to decide the sort sequence.

To sort by Activity then Surname;

View

Views

- Click on Design view
- Place the cursor over the Activity column header and the cursor should change to a small down arrow. Now click to select the column.

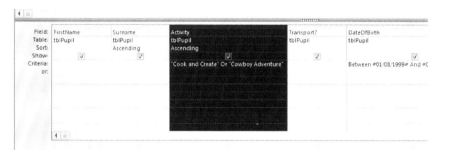

- Click and drag the grey bar at the top of the Activity column to the left of the FirstName column.

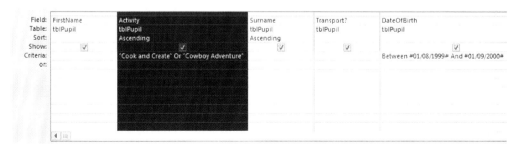

- Run the query, and you will see that the records are now sorted in the Activity then Surname order.

Run

FirstName	Activity	Surname	Transport?	DateOfBirth
James	Cook and Create	Appleton	☐	21/08/2000
Sarah	Cook and Create	Reynold	☑	28/06/2000
Sunil	Cowboy Adventure	Basu	☑	29/08/1999
Emily	Cowboy Adventure	Holden	☑	01/08/1999
*			☐	

qryCook&Cowboy

HIDING FIELDS

Suppose you decide you do not need the Transport? field in this particular report.

- Return to Design View.

View

Views

- Click on the Show box in the Transport? column to deselect it.

Field:	FirstName	Activity	Surname	Transport?	DateOfBirth
Table:	tblPupil	tblPupil	tblPupil	tblPupil	tblPupil
Sort:		Ascending	Ascending		
Show:	☑	☑	☑	☐	☑
Criteria:		"Cook and Create" Or "Cowboy Adventure"			Between #01/08/1999# And #01/09/2000#
or:					

- Run the query again. It should appear as shown below;

FirstName ▾	Activity ▾	Surname ▾	DateOfBirth ▾
James	Cook and Create	Appleton	21/08/2000
Sarah	Cook and Create	Reynold	28/06/2000
Sunil	Cowboy Adventure	Basu	29/08/1999
Emily	Cowboy Adventure	Holden	01/08/1999

- Select File, Save from the menu to save the modified query.

PRINTING YOUR QUERY

- Now, you can do a Print Preview by clicking on the File tab and selecting Print and Print Preview button. The page layout can be altered as you did with the table in Formatting and Printing in Chapter 5.
- Save and close the query.
- Close the database by selecting File, Close Database from the menu bar.

Chapter 7

PRESENTING DATA

Suppose you want to present the data in a table or query in a neater way, for example, with a proper title and date. For this you would need a Report. Reports allow you to present data in a wide variety of ways. They can be based on queries or on tables.

- Open Access and select Recent ActivitiesDatabase on the list to the right.
- Double click on the file name to open it.

MAKING A REPORT

The trip leader needs a register of all members going on the Cook and Create weekend. Remember that you created qryCookAndCreate in the last chapter, which contained only those members whose activity was Cook and Create. Our report will be based on this query.

- In the data base window, select the Create tab.
- Select the Report wizard button.

- In the tables/queries drop down list select qryCookAndCreate.

- In the box below will be a list of all the fields in the query.
  Highlight First name and click > to make it appear in the report.
- Repeat this for Surname and Transport?

We will leave Activity out of the report because we know that all the members will be doing Cook and Create.

- Click on Next

The Next dialogue box will ask about grouping levels. The youth club leader would find it useful to have the members grouped by who needs transport.

- Click Transport? So that it is highlighted, then click >
- Click Next

Now you are asked for a sort order. We want the members in Surname, then FirstName order.

- In the first drop-down list select Surname.
- In the second drop-down list select FirstName.

The next two dialogue boxes are about the format and style of the report. We will leave as they are for now.

- Click Next two more times, until Access asks What title do you want for your report?
- Enter RptCookAndCreate.
- Click on Finish

The report, saved as rptCookAndCreate, should appear as shown below;

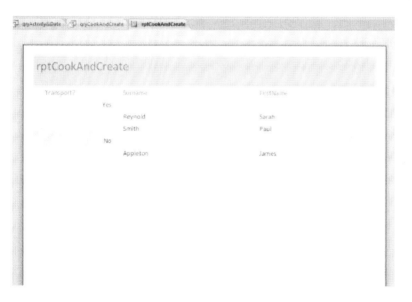

EDITING THE REPORT FORMAT

To format the report you use Design View.

Notice that in the open report the entry Yes in the Transport? Field appears too far to the right of the Transport? Title.

- Click on the Close Print Preview button.

- Make sure you are in the Design view by clicking on the Design view button.

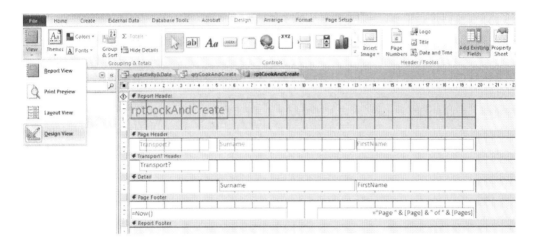

- Click in the Transport? Field (note, you want the field, not the label. The field is the one that is under the title).

- In the Format tab at the top of the screen, click on the Align left icon.

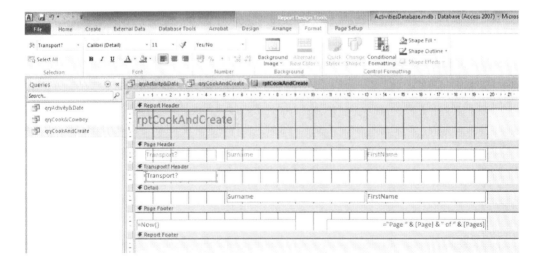

- Return to Print Preview by clicking the Home tab and selecting the Print Preview option and check that Yes appears in the right place.

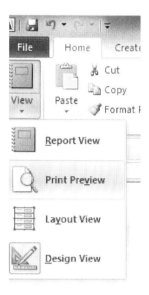

CHANGING THE TITLES

At the moment the title of the report is qryCookAndCreate. To change the title to Cook And Create Weekend;

- Return to Design View, close Print Preview.
- Click in the box that says rptCookAndCreate. Click again and the text cursor should appear in the box.

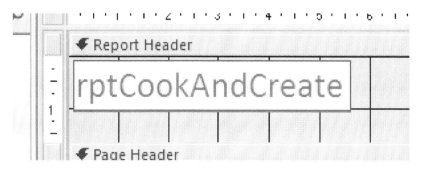

You can now edit the text.

- Change the title from rptCookAndCreate to Cook and Create Activity Weekend.

Report Header					
Cook And Create Activity Weekend					
Page Header					
Transport?		Surname		FirstName	
Transport? Header					
Transport?					
Detail					
		Surname		FirstName	
Page Footer					
=Now()				="Page " & [Page] & " of " & [Pages]	
Report Footer					

- Select the Print Preview option again and check that the report looks the way you want.

ADDING FIELDS TO THE REPORT

It would be useful, when the list of members on the Cook And Create weekend gets longer, to have a Total Field which counts the number of members on the weekend.

- Make sure the report is in Design View.

We want to put the total in the Report Footer – don't worry that there's no white page there yet.

- Click in the text box icon on the Design tab under the Report Design Tools heading. A little ab should appear by the cursor where you can add text.

- Click below the Report Footer and drag to make a rectangular field.

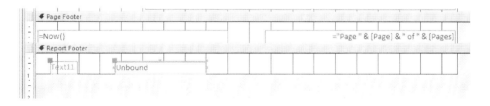

You will see that a properties wind for the text box appears. If this window does not automatically appear;

- Select the text box (the box containing Unbound).
- Click on the Properties Sheet button from the main ribbon.

- In the Properties window, the text will have a Name property something like Text 1 (the number may be different in your database).

You may need to select the border of the properties window to drag it to the left to read all the information

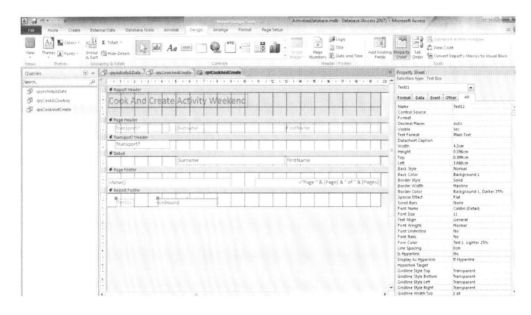

- Change the name of the Text box to Total
- In the Control Source property enter =Count(*). This counts the number of records in the report, which equals the number of people on the Activities Weekend.

- Click on the Text11 label on the report, then click again to edit the text. Change it to say Total.

- Return to Print Preview to check the results

If you would like to tidy up the appearance of the report, you can return to Design View and change fonts, add lines and do various other things using the format tab at the top of the screen.

PRINTING YOUR REPORT

- In Print Preview click the Print icon.

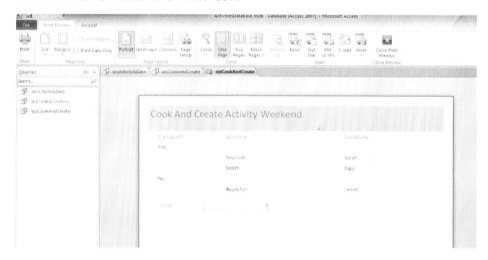

- Save and close your Report.

CREATING A PIE CHART

It is possible to create a report that represents selected information as a graph. Although this sounds complicated, it is easy to create a simple graph using the Chart tool.

We will create a chart to show the number of members taking each activity.

- In the database window, select the Create tab and select the icon Report Design. This creates a blank report.

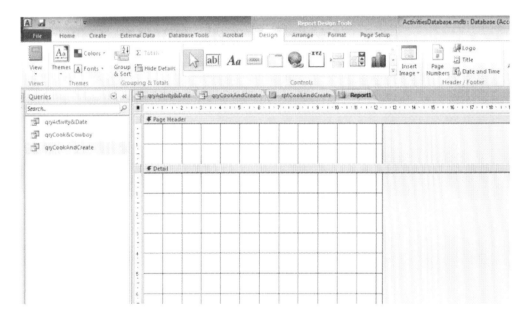

- Select the Chart icon and draw a large box section on the detail of the report.
- In the new Chart wizard dialogue box, select tblPupil.

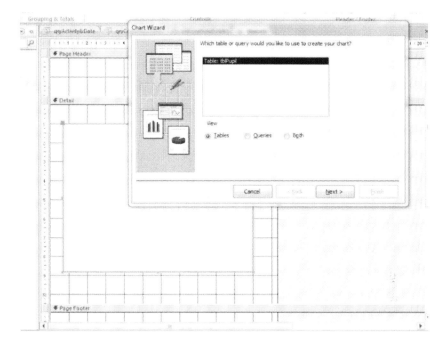

- Click on Next.

- Select Activity from the list of on the left.

- Press > so that the field appears under Fields for Chart on the right.

- Click on Next.

Now you are given a choice of several different types of graph. For this example, a pie chart is a good way of presenting the information.

- In access, bar charts are called Column Charts, Column Charts should already be selected in the top left of the window,

- Select the pie Chart and click on Next.

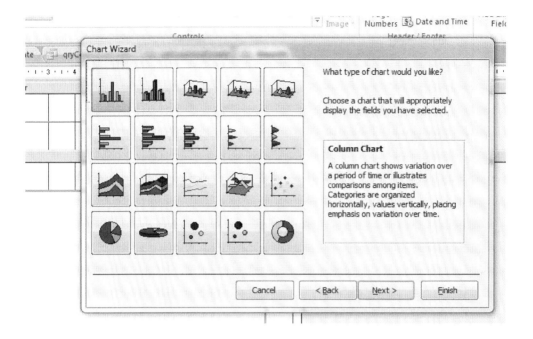

- In the next window, the graph is automatically set out how we would like, so just click Next.

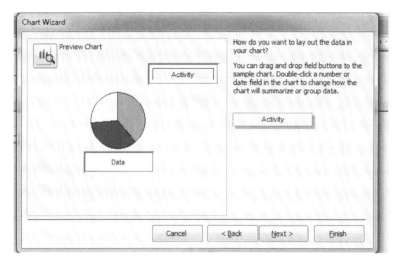

- Type Activities Chart as the title for your report.

- Click on Finish

- Your Chart should now appear as a Print Preview

CREATING A BAR CHART

Now let's try a bar chart. A bar Chart shows the same information as a pie chart but in a different form. We are going to do this another way. This is a way of editing and moving data around to display charts in a variety of ways.

- Click on the Create tab and select More forms to make the drop-down menu appear as shown below.

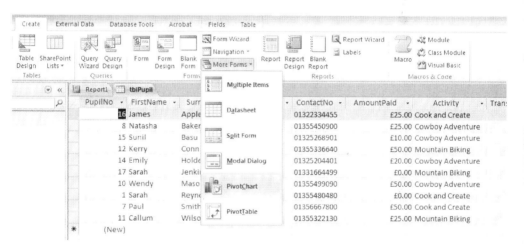

- Select Pivot Chart
- Double click on the Field List button to show you the fields from the table that was open.
- Drag the Activity field onto the data section highlighted in blue below.

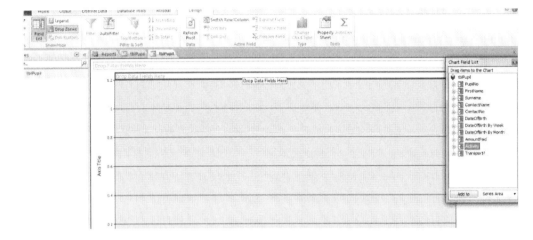

- Now drag Activity on the categories box

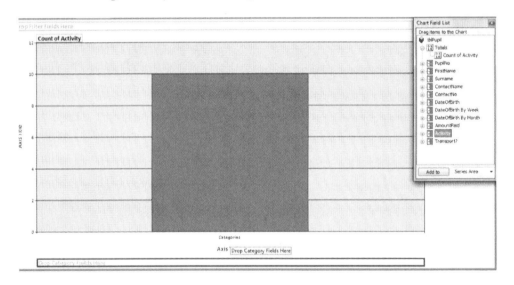

- Your Bar chart should look like this.

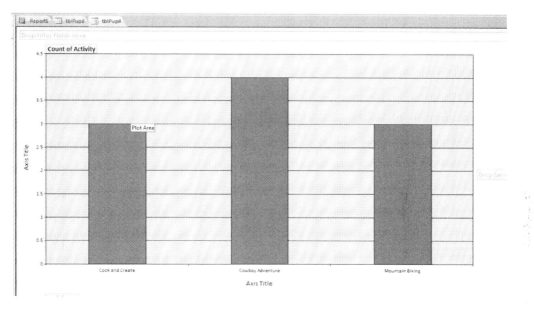

- Click on the Drop Zones button to remove the Drop zones.

- Enter sensible Axis titles.
- Save your Chart.

If you make a mistake in your chart it is possible to edit it in Design View, but it's probably easier just to start the Chart again.

Chapter 8

Forms are used to create a 'user interface'. They allow database users to type data into a database using a specially designed form, rather than straight into a table.

As well as providing an easy way of entering data, you can also tailor forms to accept only certain information, or only information in the correct format. This is another method of data validation.

CREATING A FORM

We will create a form to enter all the members and their details. This form will be used for entering data into the tblPupil table.

- In the database window, click on create and select Form Wizard.

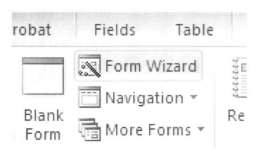

- In the Tables/Queries drop-down list select Table: tblPupil.

- The box below contains all the fields in the tblPupil. We want all the fields to appear on the form, so press >> to move all the fields to the Selected Fields box on the right.
- Click on Next. Leave the layout as Columnar, and click Next again.
- Save the form as frmPupil and click on Finish.

Your form should appear like this one;

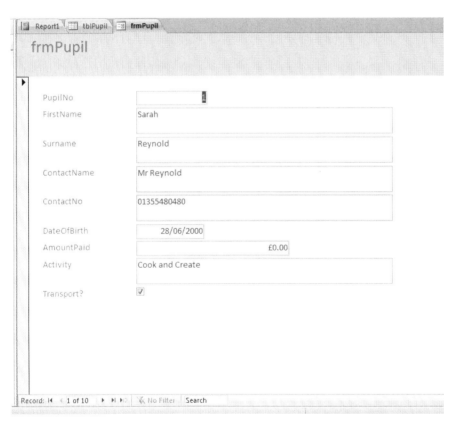

The form contains all the records that are already entered in tblPupil. To switch between records use the record selectors at the bottom of the form. Move your cursor over each button and a description will appear after a few seconds.

ENTERING A RECORD USING THE FORM

- Using the record selectors, click the New Record icon.

A blank form will be displayed.

- Enter the following pupil. Use the tab key to move to the next field.

FirstName	Surname	ContactName	ContactNo	DateOfBirth	Activity	Amount Paid	Transport?
Paul	Brash	Mr Brash	01687435869	16/8/2000	Mountain Biking	£5	Y

MAKING DATA ENTRY QUICKER

Since there are only 3 choices of activity, it would be convenient to select the activity from a drop-down list.

There are two options here;

A list box shows a box on screen displaying some or all the options (no drop-down list)

Or

A Combo box shows just one value at a time. To view all the options you click in the box to view the drop-down list.

We will use a Combo box.

COMBO BOXES

- Go to design View by clicking the Design View button.
- Make the form about twice as wide by dragging out the right border.
- Click the Combo Box icon in the ribbon under the design tab.

Click about a field's width to the right of the Activity field, and drag out a rectangle.

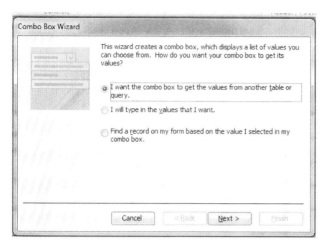

- Select the middle option I will type in the values that I want.

- Click Next

- Leave the number of columns as 1. In the box below type in the activities; Mountain biking, Cook And Create, Cowboy Adventures.

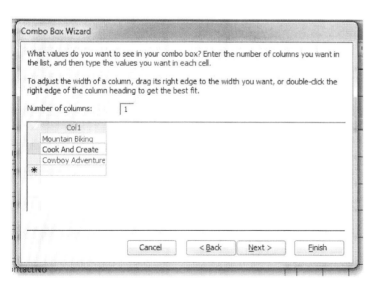

- Click Next. In the next box, select Store that value in this field and choose Activity as the field from the drop-down list.

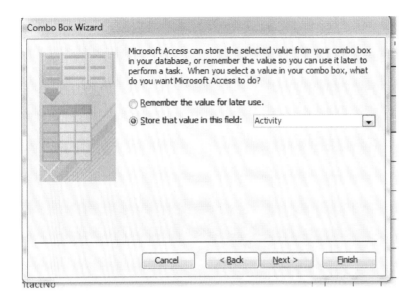

- Click Next. Set the Name of the Combo box to Activity and click on Finish.

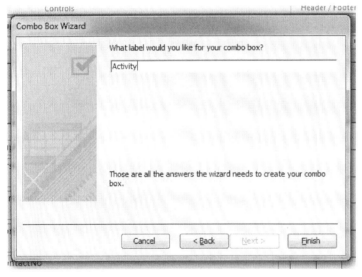

- Click on the old Activity field and press the Delete key. Both the field and the label will disappear.

- Move the combo box and its label into place by clicking them once, then clicking and dragging the border.

- Click the Form View button.

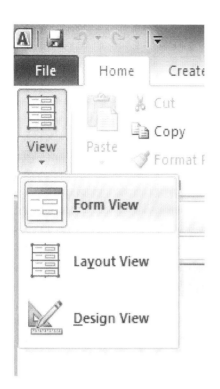

- You can now see there is a drop-down list containing all activities. Click its Down arrow to show them.

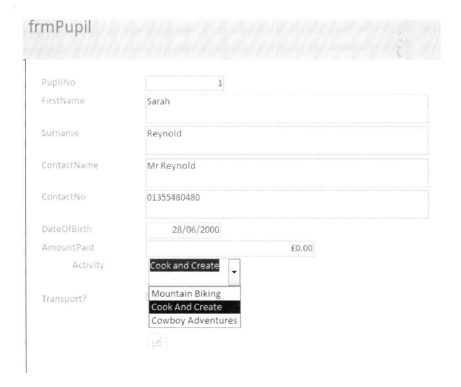

SETTING A DEFAULT VALUE

You can specify values for fields before the user has typed anything. For example, since most pupils require transport, it would make sense to make the default Yes.

- Go to Design View
- If the Properties dialogue box is not already open, open it by clicking the Properties Sheet button in the Design tab ribbon.
- Click on the Transport? Field on the form and the Properties box should display the properties of this filed (makes sure you have selected the field not the label).

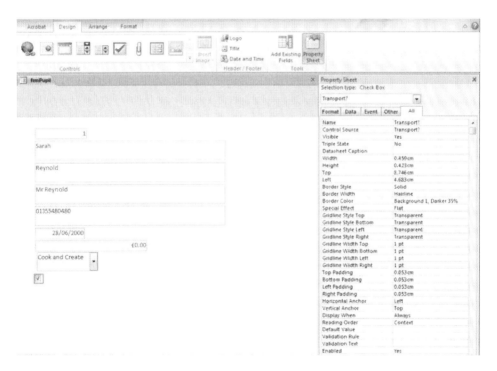

- In the Default Value row in the Properties window, type Yes.

Gridline Width Right	1 pt
Top Padding	0.053cm
Bottom Padding	0.053cm
Left Padding	0.053cm
Right Padding	0.053cm
Horizontal Anchor	Left
Vertical Anchor	Top
Display When	Always
Reading Order	Context
Default Value	Yes ...
Validation Rule	

- Go to Form View

- Click the New Record icon on the Form Design ribbon

You are going to enter a new record using the features you have just added.

- Enter the following member into the form;

FirstName	Surname	ContactName	ContactNo	DateOfBirth	Activity	AmountPaid	Transport
Katie	Sapsford	Mrs Sapsford	013255 657899	28/5/2001	Mountain Biking	£20	Y

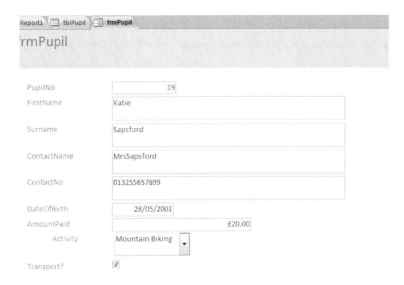

There's still a bit of tidying up you could do on your form. Some fields don't need to be as wide, and the labels would be better right-aligned.

- Save and close the from when your happy with it.
- Click on the File tab and Close the database. Save and changes if you are prompted to do so.

WELL DONE! THAT'S IT, NOW YOU KNOW THE BASICS OF MICROSOFT ACCESS 2010 AND DATABASES.

26698563R00067

Printed in Poland
by Amazon Fulfillment
Poland Sp. z o.o., Wrocław